i'll see you tomorrow,
a collection of poems about growing up and growing out.

Cecelia Allentuck

Copyright © 2024: Cecelia Allentuck
All Rights Reserved. ISBN: 979-8-89324-241-6
Printed in the United States of America.

No part of this publication shall be reproduced, transmitted, or sold in whole or in part in any form without prior written consent of the author, except as provided by the United States of America copyright law. Any unauthorized usage of the text without express written permission of the publisher is a violation of the author's copyright and is illegal and punishable by law. all trademarks and registered trademarks appearing in this guide are the property of their respective owners.

The opinions expressed by the author are not necessarily those held by Publishers.

Dedicated to:

*To those with their heads in the clouds,
To Patti, my parents, and my friends,
Thank you for being the reason I write.*

"We don't read and write poetry because it's cute. We read and write poetry because we are members of the human race."
— ***Mr. Keating,***
The Dead Poets' Society

Bye, love you–

"Spring is here! Why doesn't the breeze delight me?"
*– **Rodgers & Hart***

A Seed for Every Sorrow

When the trees I grew up with
Were torn down,
I knew my childhood had been chopped up
With them, to be used
As wood, fueling fireside chats
Of the 'good-old-days' and
Molding in the heat of summer.
The Oak on Main Street is gone,
Just in front of the town hall–
No stump to remember its age,
As ringless as my old school's bell
When the rope became too frayed to pull.

Every day, I biked past–
Watched kids climb,
Watched them fall,
Watched bugs and ants and bees
Swarm its trunk,
Saw squirrels and birds and seeds
Build their homes in the burrows
Of my youth–
     Once built upon a future of uncertainty
Held within the caress of the natural world.

I have no way to climb the sprawling limbs,
Look out on the horizon
And know
I will find solace in the growing saplings:
     The aching stems, stretching toward the sun
I hide from.

If it can't see me,
It cannot know
That I am afraid.

Afraid like I was when that old tree–
Across the street–
Was taken from me.
Watched with empty regard every second it stood,
It so quickly became the staple of
A whole life,
Holding together every piece of me
I was afraid to lose.

I lost the shade of a backyard.
To the snowstorm and its dusting.
Now, there is only
A blizzard of heat.

And all that's left are seeds.

Empty promises I'll never get to see,
Lifetimes that will never belong to me,
And I am expected to
Just go with it.

To find them, plant them,
And watch them grow–
Expected to understand the circle of life:
    The tree must fall at the hands of Man
    Man must fall at the hands of the Universe
    And the Universe must play its tricky little games

Until I see everything
Clearly,
In the light,
And by then, I will watch the seed

Become seedling,
Stretch toward the sun
And view beyond the horizon,

But for now,
I'll walk through the empty space,
Wondering

What in the world
Could make me want to leave this town?

Everything We Built Will Burn

I am seventeen now, and the days go by quicker
Because I take up more space within them.
I still spend the late nights laughing
Into dark shadows
So that light might appear with each
Breath, shaking off the tip of my tongue.
But now, I fear I'll wake the next generation,
Reliving my childhood
As my friends and I run
Yelling through the streets,
Mosquitoes sipping our blood
In their own sweet victory.
But I find that this moment is worth the itch.
Our minds have yet to develop,
So we don't look back as we race.
One day,
When our brains solidify,
And stop rolling around inside
Our heads, grown too large for our bodies
To carry like they once had–

We will look back and see a road,
Long, dark, and barren
But at the end,
A light appears,
As bubbling laughter fills the night air.

Summer Chorus

I wish to match nature
To both wear sparkly pink shoes
As we enter the next stage of our lives–
Kicking and dancing
Because,
I always wanted light up sneakers
But they never fit my sapling leaves
And now my tree trunk feet are much too large
To walk like a child's
Down a wood path,
As I search stems for bugs
And rocks for toads.

I will never again know
My beginning.
My cycles spin with the strike of
Lightning in summer–
The capricious nature of the natural world
Where thunder is the applause
Of this grand performance
That has always felt
Real, authentic
And now I am forgetting my lines.

How can I forgive myself for giving up
This early?
Before the tenth anniversary of my eighth birthday?
The day my life ended,

Because I was one year older,
And a year later,
It began again.
And so it goes.

In a cycle, rhythmic flow of a river
Brought to the sea
Brought to a new river.

There is no end
And there is no beginning.

But perhaps,
There are sparkly pink shoes in my future
And matching pj bottoms
As I go to sleep with the sun,
Sparkling and pink,
And wake with the birds
Singing morning songs,
Outside my window.

Watering Can

I miss being a little girl,
When things were easier–
–I would pick weeds,
Earthbound seeds–
Growing in the garden
Spinning whirlwind in the sky.

Now, I pick flowers
That grow out of my own head.
I place them face down,
Until they leave an imprint
Bringing stains where I lay,
Colors painting petals
That have begun to wilt.

Writing By Candlelight

During the winter, I shed my glow,
Step out of my bare feet,
Take the flowers, one by one, from my hair.
The locks fall heavy against my shoulders,
My bones ache with a want for the sun,
My eyes close, skin sagging with the shadows
Cast by the candlelight.
The Earth spins and the world progresses,
But I sit in wait,
Hibernating.

I follow the life of the tree outside my window–
Growing, growing, growing
Until its branches snap in the wind,
And it must start all over again.
The snow buries my flower petals,
And turns bright yellow to gray.
Below me, the grass hardens
To weather the storms,
And I muster my strength to prepare
For the shortened days, which
Deprive me of drinking the sun's golden elixir.
My youth escapes me in the winter.
If I chase it, I lose my breath and
Hunch over, rooting in place,
Grounded in wait.
As the trees die,
The plants lay limp,

The birds fly away,
The bugs disintegrate,
And I, still in wait,
Work myself to sleep

Slumbering in my cave,
As the cold wraps me in a blanket
Of faux warmth.

Slip

Remind me to stop being a woman.
I can only break so many times
To stitch myself back together again.
I can only bleed and forget last months
Knife, sinking into my stomach.
Blade meets bone and I am cut to pieces.
Fingers hold me up by the bra straps,
Snapping into place
A fragility I haven't felt since I scraped my knee
So many years ago
When being a little girl
Meant pigtails and slumber parties.

But now I am stranded in the middle of the street

I grew up crossing, looking both ways,
In the learned habits of staying safe.

But now I am stranded in the middle of the street.

On one side: womanhood,
A dress I must step into, zip from the waist up
And feel pinching at my hips.
On the other side: girlhood.

Where I am still blowing out candles
For my seventeenth birthday party.

I have to fit the mold of the woman I am meant to be
But it has not yet been made.
The ground grows cold beneath my feet
As frost bites my toes.
I wish it were possible to remain, just a little while longer,
Here.

As My Hair Thins

I am an oak tree
Who has not yet grown into her bark.

Instead, I soak my leaves
In the rainwater,
Let them sag and drip and
Spill to the dirt below.

I know one day,
My muted breeze
Will be heard,
Cast in the rustle of my
Bristling branches, no longer
Weighed down by snow.
I know one day,
My roots will not grow tired,
Stretching to connect with my neighbors.
I know one day,
I will breathe in real peace
Instead of just oxygen.

I know that one day, I will watch
As every tree in this forest falls,
I know one day my center will not ache
When the crash adds one more ring
To my swollen tree trunk,
Bulging out from termite-ridden holes.

I know one day,
This bark will no longer itch.
One day,
I will not fear the expanse of sky

That grows shorter as I enter it,
And wider as it comes into view.

One day,
When I can see over the canopy.
One day,
When I forget the splintering stumps below.
One day,
When my bark feels as light as the sun's rays.

Lost, Unfound

Body bruised from the places I battle it,

Broken, black, and blue from empty paint bottles
Used to make a smile.

Make it shimmer.

I cannot go unseen, and yet I cloak myself
In smiles, shimmering.

I have to be heard, and yet I hold my throat,
Tight lips in a smile, shimmering.

To grow, I need dreams
Other than breaking,
Other than buying brand new bones
Bundled in a pack of six–
Six promises in one stack.
It didn't used to be like this.

Fallacies used to be a joke
Cracked at the dinner table.
Now empty plates sit shattered,
Their ceramic smiles – shimmering –

I cannot remember the last time
I stared into the mirror
And didn't hate what I saw.

Thawed ice – shimmering – at the corners,
But it was clear enough to see
That the body most disgraced,
Was the one belonging to me.

Head dancing above the waves,
Hailstorm floods in the trenches,
Every battle fought was in vain.

I lost every time.
And it didn't used to be like this.

I would run home,
Gap toothed from where I knocked out
The front two,
Smiling, shimmering,
With a medal strung
Around my neck
For being the nicest.

The smile has become a decoration,
The shimmer now a mere glare.

I use a wrench,
Found in a box of old tools,
To tighten all my loose bolts,
But, again, they come undone.

I twist and twist and twist
As the sweat pours down my cheeks.

It will never get easier.
When the body is broken, it is too valuable to buy
Used parts,
So I am stuck with the ones rusting.

As time surges forward:
I cry out, sword raised – shimmering –
And the battle continues on.

The First Adventure

I smell it before I see it.

But when the smoke entrails
Twirl through the air, dancing
The way between the stranger and me,

I am taken back to the car,
The white of the Jeep, dirty from age,
The seats I don't remember the
Feel or look of–
Which I neglected to memorize–

Never have I so strongly
Felt the scent wash over my
Skin, taking me back to the
Endless drive home,
Which I could trace each step of
Only to find how short the path

Until I am back here, in stone walkways,
Pale buildings built by hand,
Small, cramped breakfasts

And the sticky hands washed in orange juice

Bringing me back to sticky fingers, sticky smiles–
Sticky summers I am stuck with the memories of.

When bathing suits fit and ice cream didn't melt,
When she woke me in the morning with doughnuts
And held me through swollen lip tears,

Reminding me to sit still on this hilltop
Of a foreign place we never knew–
– but now I feel –

And I didn't expect her to be everywhere here.

Not in the bees, cozying themselves up
On the shooting grass
Itching my legs

And suddenly, I am taken all the way back,
Melting in all her summers,
All her school days,

She would sit on the steps waiting,
1,000 miles away.
But I feel her steadying me in every piece of stone
Beneath my laced up shoes.

When I get home, she will not be there waiting,
Cigarette hanging limply from her fingertips,
As I tell her
Smoking will kill you,
And now I fear it might kill me,
As I soak up the last remains of her.

When I get home, she will not be there waiting,
So I stay here longer, understanding

There will be no swollen lips, just salty tears
No fresh oranges to peel, just sticky grief to sit in
There will be no silhouette of her face,
Twirling in the air, just a fingertip's touch away.

The smoke lingers here,
It smells, it sticks,

It brings me back to her.

I stand behind the stranger
One moment longer.
I breathe smoke in,
I breathe it out,
And I cross the road

Only to feel her linger.

Seventeen

An unfinished poem
Unpublished, unseen
Anticipating an end but scared all the same
Feeling everything, and yet, numb to the pain

I don't think there's ever been an age
More conditioned to feel loss,
Expect gain, and yet continue on.

I vow to whine,
I lose my mind,
And yet, continue on.

On and on, off and on,
A cycle where I am caught on step one,
Silver lining the edges of my
Teenage angst, they say is just a phase

But it has followed me all the way from birth,
Wedged itself into the hearth of my
Blazing coals, raging blue
With an unexpected burn.

There is no heat for my chilled landmarks,
Rejected by their earned worth.
Left beat, right to the core

Sore, torn and tattered–
Seventeen and sixteen and all the in betweens
That got me here.

Splattered paint on an empty canvas,
I fill the space, unclean, and feel

Unsatisfied, led by the urge
To do more.
To be more.

But I am seventeen and stuck in place,
Paused in motion:

A thought, the quotient of my divided soul.
A dream, the revival of faces unknown.
A goal, the second hand of a grandfather clock.
The future, a house of mirrors

Nothing has ever been clearer
And yet, I run into every wall I see,
Too afraid to climb over them.
Every day, I believe

It can get better,

But I am only seventeen–
Stupid, happy, free,
Caged, afraid, lost in my dreams.
Frostbitten skin, sinking.
Sunburned, rimmed with gold.

One day, I'll unfold,
Unfurl and behold the pages
That got me here–

But for now,
I am a semicolon,
Placed where I see fit.

I look within myself, feel without consequence,

And hope that I will always feel seventeen,

Sixteen,
And everything in between,

I breathe in, breathe out
Fear the loudness of my mind,
Find every excuse to silence it.

When I listen and lose myself in the chaos,
I am reminded of when everything seemed
An extended deadline.

Light trickles in and my mild memories flash.
I remember beams of light
And little bright spots that
I do not see anymore

Because everything is closer.
Everything closes in on me.
So I remain unfinished;

Good for My Age

It is so hard to be,
Anything besides who people see me as.

On the rise as a real person
And my potential seems to seep out
With every second I am not doing
Something.

Something remarkable,
Something of note,
Something beyond my years.

I can only stay ahead for so long
So what happens when time catches up?

In the dull moments,
In the expanding silences,
In the birthdays that keep appearing quicker
With each year I age.

Only my words stick,
But what happens when they are erased?

Who will I be when the eyes
Shift to the next generation,
Mouths open wide, a sigh of fresh air,

As I grow into the wrinkles around my mouth,
And become too old to impress
And too average to exist as they expect me to?

Sleeping Without Stuffed Animals

Sometimes I feel so brave.

When I take the plane alone or
Speak up in a doctor's appointment.
When I make new friends and
Tell my parents about them.

But there is still that little girl within me,
Who still fears walking through the dark and
Keeps the bedroom door open a crack,

It all makes me giggle sometimes.
How I can be old enough to drive a car,
But I still need to look back and make sure
My mom is behind me in the grocery store.

All this little hand holding makes me wonder
What bravery will look like in a few years.
What will be an accomplishment and what

Will be expected of me?

I wish I could scream, shout into my pillow
And know that my dad will be there
In the flip of a switch
To turn the lights on.

I think it is okay to be crazy sometimes

Even if the tears stain my cheeks,
And there is no one to wipe them away.

Blank

I am so unremarkable
That I am stained with red
Polka dots
To remind me
How dull I can really be.
I stick out in a crowd–
The Picasso among Van Gohs
The Thomas Cole among Monets.

No one looks at me and understands.

They don't find beauty in my watery eyes
Or technique in my sad smile.

Visuals will never do the trick for me.

So I stick to words.
Only when my Plath nature
Obtrudes their Elizabethan sonnets,
I am once again
Unremarkable.

Because it is one thing to be sad and complex,
But it is another to be sad and empty.

So I'll paint pictures with my words.
White canvas splattered with eraser marks,
Blown from the table's edge.

No one will ever see me appear in brighter tones
As I remain stuck in my artistry,
Afraid to show the world that

I am afraid of living alone.

If someone were to find me,
I would draw a dot on paper and
Write their name above it.

Then, they would see
Plain and simple,
Beauty unremarkably.

We All Fade In The End

I've learned,
Sunshine is limited.

Fields roll and roll until they roll away,
And the grasses that fill the prairie fry
Beneath the glare of the sun,
And the sun,
Eventually,
Runs out of power.
No Triple A batteries will fill its center.

The Earth's core will melt and dissolve.
The crust will evaporate.
The life we have built will fall in a sweep of
Ashes, blown away by a gasp. Delicately
Balanced on the edge of this cliff–

One foot dances off the rocks

It twists and cracks and twists and cracks
And twists and cracks until
The pop doesn't phase me

And the gentle release of air between my joints
Does not fill the empty spaces spreading
Through a once bountiful body–

I am lost
Wounded in the desert, searching for water,
Stung by acid rain,
Sitting in a taxi at the heart of the city,
Trying to find faces I recognize but only seeing

The same street sign again and again and
Again and,
Climbing a redwood that has no leaves.

They have all been shed for the winter,
They have all drifted to the ground to be
Disintegrated and digested by worms,
Bellies full on laughter and chlorophyll–

I want to be as dead as the dirt

Because then maybe my cycle of life
Would have meaning.
I want to streamline water through my body
And not flush that feeling,
I want to cover secrets and uncover gold,
I want to be

Cold and warm and wretched and dirty and scruffed
And by all means busy!

Bees buzz and bury my desires,
Stinging with poison as sweet as my blood–

I'll drink to childhood wishes and broken promises,
Drunk on adolescent dreams and
High on sidewalk chalk.
The scent of cinnamon follows me home,

Where I lay, pretending fresh bread is
There, waiting in the oven for me.

Advice

They always tell you,
    You'll grow up.
But they never warn you,
That one day,
You will grow out–

Out
Of the bonfires,
And the s'mores, burning your fingers
Of the movie nights,
On the couch, under the covers
Of the slumber parties
Of staying up past midnight
Of reading until you're drowning in words
Of fall leaves on the pavement,
Shaping the world in blurred lines of color
Of Halloween costume contests
And drives to school and counting games

Of feeling like this small town is so big
The rest of the world might as well not even exist–

When did I grow out of it all?

Snow days used to sparkle,
Magic in the dragon's breath blow of cold air,
In the penguin huddles at the top of a hill,
Just before the quick descent to the bottom,
Where a chill creeps up your spine

Because you will never exist,
Cheeks rosy with winter air,
In this moment again.
We were a snow globe shaken
Just before the powder settled to the bottom.

But now there is work to catch up on,
Deadlines to meet that make the weeks
Feel like days
And summers feel like pools of ice cream
Melting between the cracks in the pavement.

The sun once dipped my smile in honey,
But now it sinks low,
Draining energy from both the world
And my body,
Placing the remains on a high shelf
I cannot grow tall enough to reach.

I don't want to leave this cell,
For it is all I have ever known as home,
But there is a bigger world out there–

Isn't there?

Don't I have the right to know what it feels like–
Again, to be growing up,
Growing in

To something new, something so divine
I fill my lungs with its promises.

I want to grow in again,
But first, I must grow out,

And that is much more painful
Than they will ever tell you,
Because growing out
Means leaving behind

Every ounce of yesterday
In order to feel the warmth of tomorrow's sun.

I find it when I wake in the morning,
Dazzling in my head as though the rest was all

Some distant dream.

see you tomorrow -

"So make the friendship bracelets, take the moment and taste it, you've got no reason to be afraid."
– Taylor Swift

the wind carries me

Deep within me,
There are colors of another creature

Whom I fear I'll never get to meet.

I knock on the door,
Call in through the threshold,
But no one ever answers.

Its remains
Stain the world around me
In little blurs, images of a distant land,
Picturesque reminders that

There is more to come.

And yet, I am stuck in this
Wobbly in-between:

The moments of silence after lightning,
Before thunder.
The spaces between stone as a mountain
Gets higher, steeper, and harder to climb.
The split second of a butterfly's closed wings.

I wind down this narrow path and
Begin to wonder,

Is it too late to turn back?

This creature within me,

Aches, begs to be freed.

My feet itch to run,
My fingers burn to

Pick every flower in a field.

Colors, colors, and more colors!
Bright as the ray of light shining down from the sun,
There is no more creature within me
If I let it prowl my deepest desires,
Let it sink its teeth into every dream
My mind has ever explored.
It lets loose, wreaks havoc on this world
And I find,
There is no harm to be done

In living through a deeper lens.

I mend the tear in my side,
Stitch up my hollow abdomen and watch
The colors flood my vision.

It is happening, I believe,

I am beginning to understand
What it means to truly live!

the light feeds me

I believe I am a failure
And no one can tell me otherwise.

The trees' acorns fall without doubt.
The squirrels hide them but
Never remember where they dug.

In the fall, in the soil, the Earth is still warm
In the winter, in the snow, the path freezes over

I dig and dig and dig
Until I find a patch of water
And sip the blood of Mother Nature.
Lifting cupped hands to my chapped lips,

I sip and sip and sip
Until my fingers grow numb
Until my hair dries, unwashed
Until my eyes sting with salt,

I sip and sip and sip
Until I am pushed into the hole
I dug for myself–

Beneath the cold dirt, I find
A single acorn top, soaked
And broken in half, two

Pieces of acorn in my hand,
On the palm, where lines intersect
Between my fingers, unfeeling,
And back into the hole
For a squirrel to forget and find one day.

I look up,
I see someone standing there,
She's got brown, curly hair
And a bright smile, blinding.

I look into her eyes,
I see flecks of gold,
I see a flash of silver,
I see a stream of liquid,

I watch her cry,

From above, she whispers,
"You are not a failure",
And before I can deny her words,
My frostbitten figure laced in disbelief,

The walls of my hole are pressing in.

She covers me with a blanket of
Warm soil, and the bugs sing for me,

They sing me to sleep
And when I open my eyes,
I am rooted in the ground,

My fingers dance above my head
Until I feel the fresh spring air
Tickling them, taunting them,

As I sprout,
And grow,
And become.

listen, she awakes

The sun mounts the world
On its silver axis
And no longer do I feel like Atlas.

The weight of the clouds,
Heavy with rainwater and anger.
The piles of leaves,
Dripping in the lost dreams hidden within them.
The push and pull of the wind,
Singing lullabies to help me step
Off of this pedestal.

They all crumble into pebble, into sand,
In drops of water,
Sinking to the ground,
Streaming through the cracks
Of this budding society.

And the sun!
It lifts its golden chariot to the sky,
Shouting to the reigns,
Shining down on my shoulders
And releasing them of their tension–

Conversations always feel like a prayer
At this hour.
Whispering, I stand in awe
Of what the day might behold.

flowering

When she takes me to the trees,
I climb the branch she extends
And sit there for a good few hours,

Watching the birds and the bees explore the air

As I explore the Earth.
When she wraps me in her leaves,
I am full to the brim with oxygen

Waiting for the sun to drop
Waiting for the flowers to wilt
Waiting for the world to stop turning
Waiting in the branches of her tree.

When they do not,
I search within,

Within the trunk,
A family of beetles carve their own community
Between old and young,
Dead and just freshly sprouted from
The spools of the universe, tightly threaded,

It is the kind of magic only a tree could behold,
A spell cast, transforming suffocation
Into exhalation,

A message to the world,
That it is all going to be okay.

glass half empty, glass half full

Who taught me how to love?

     Morning croissants (Pillsbury from the bottle) and shopping for sweets when Dad went
Out of town

Taught me how to love

     Quick turnarounds for funeral shoes and watermelon runs after school when exhaustion
     Settles in

Taught me how to love

     Late night studying, drowning in tears of confusion, long walks in the dark, lit up and glowing from the
Gentle flow of voices

Taught me how to love

     Hugs and kisses after seven years separate, curls tangling to create one messy-haired monster
     Who fights doubt

With love

     Snack money and back rubs, the world around me enters a quiet slumber, but like the river,
     Our easy flow will always remain the same

    Flowers in the crook of an elbow, when doubt
knocks on my door and polaroid pictures
shut it out

Hiking when the sun is setting, when my energy levels lessen
    Reading the clock that makes me tick and not
thinking it strange
    How many metaphors I use for the names of feelings
I wish to convey

Taught me how to love

    Sledding and snowball fights
    And the snowwomen we make, whose names
we cannot agree on
    Study sessions with my favorite popcorn
salty, stale, serene
    Laughter from the belly, when books are
worlds we enter
    Hand in hand

Taught me how to love

    Songs about the moon,
singing instead of screaming
    Waking up to the car's exhaust as it parks in
the driveway that burns my bare feet
In the summertime

Taught me how to love

I dance when the record scratches,
Because no song has ever met me and been
Unagreeable

I was never taught to love
Through a roadmap, but held by
Warm hands as I was led blindly through the world

What taught me how to love

>	Is who taught me how to be
>	Wholly and perfectly myself

What taught me how to love

>	Was the beauty of the imperfect
>	Reminding me that when all else fails

Love presses on–

slide

Being a woman means to me–

> Body rolls at sixteen
> And walking along that beam
> That is boys pining, then
> Bending backwards
> To avoid me

> It's spinning around
> Hair flapping like a Greek Goddess
> It's frolicking in a brand new dress,

Letting it wave its wild mane

> It's going to the gym, lifting weights
> It's studying all night to ace that test
> It's glowing inside-out at three in the morning

And smiling even after ignoring all the signs and
Losing yourself in your own mind

> It's not cutting the scene just because it's boring,
> And it's body rolls at sixteen,
> When I am still wondering what being a woman

Means to me.

i float away, onward

The ocean is empty–

If not full of limbs.

Aching hip, sore knees
Fingers tired from pinching at
Bulging skin,
Cheeks red from prodding eyes
On little bumps, invisible scars

The ocean is full
Of my insecurities laced in delicate
Seaweed, sticking softly to my
Freshly shaven legs

And there is peace in this bounty–
In rolling waves,
Which chill my warm skin;
In fog, stretching across the horizon,
Clearing the air and blurring my senses.

And there are no sharks
Where I would expect them,
The jagged rocks don't bruise
My feet, sensitive from years of overuse–
My toes sink into the sand

Without burying beneath,
And I find peace in this bounty

Of limb and muscle and joint

And beauty beyond breaking points

Where the foamy, salty seawater
Meets rocky, sandy shoreline.

I float where the water meets my chest,
Stare into the sky,
And fill the ocean
With my breath, as steady as the waves
Carrying me back and forth

Between land and sea

my favorite sweatshirt, somewhere in the laundry of a friend's house

Pockets of joy,
Which I pull from in moments of lapse:

    When the storm is too loud to dance to
    When the fire is too hot to roast marshmallows in
    When the river is too dry to drink from

Pockets of joy

    In the smiles of strangers
    In the walking sticks that guide us
Down straight paths, lined in
Fresh air and grass-paved fields

Pennies from people who turn

    Hours into adventures,
Burning beauty into the mixtape of our plainness

    Where millions reside,
There is only money
    Where moments remain,
There is life.

grief in its teenage years

The shadow still sits beside me
As I curl up beneath the covers,
Late into the night, when my body's battery
Has been drained
And I cannot ignore
The skeletons, whose bones
Rattle in my closet.

We sit across from each other.
Holding hands.
Letting the silence speak for us.

It has been like this for some years now–
Four and a half, and still counting
Enough time for the mold to creep onto stone and
The grass to outgrow our memories,

Shading her from me, so that all that's left
Is the shadow–

The silhouette dancing in the dark
Meeting me in the hours I spend
Wondering who I am going to be.

The moon seeps through the blinds
And illuminates the room,
Exposing the empty space I speak to,

I would blush in the daytime, but here
It is too dark to see the color build and fade,
So I don't bother.

The moon listens to our conversation,

But I don't mind,

I have never been interrupted here,
Never made to feel like my words are as shallow
As the rivers we wade through,
Cold water rushing over our toes
As we lift our pant legs and race to the other side,

If only it were as easy
As bearing the chill and laughing through
The numbness from our feet up.

Tonight, the moon listens and adds in
When I question: where am I going?

Though the shadow simply nods along,
As she always does,

Tonight, the moon speaks to me:

Where I go, it shall follow.
And though my question remains unanswered,
I feel as though the current in my bloodstream
Has slowed to a smooth trickle,

And I find it easy to drift off,
As the moon watches over my shadow
And lets her stay with me,
Deep into the dawn.

I wipe the morning haze from my brow,
Watching fog gather on the street below.

Hello World, I whisper, where will I go today?

The shadow remains silent, but follows me

Throughout the day.
Occasionally, she tugs at my sleeve, and I

Must sit down to speak the sorrows out of her.

But my sleeves are growing thicker,
Their woven thread, sturdier.

She walks beside me now.
And waits until tonight,
When I will address my letters to her
And send them off,
Dazzling under the moon's gentle caress.

loitering

There is only so much time left.

The alarm clock wakes me in the morning
Just as I instructed it to,
And I find that independence is not as hollow
As I expected it to feel.

The wood feels sturdy this morning.
The bed–
–crumpled sheets forming the shapes
of animals where my friends used to sleep–
Is imprinted with my own body.
I shake it clean before dressing for the day.

The same pair of shorts
Is the most comfortable feeling
I will ever know.

Because even when all else tightens
Around my neck, pressing
Deep into my larynx–
–forcing out words empty of meaning–
I can make it through the day,

But I am tired of surviving.

I am tired of working ten times harder
To reap ten times less–
–weeds that continue growing

no matter how many times I have pulled them
begin to take over my garden
and fill my room, housing bugs that

leave footprints all over my bare skin
leaving me to itch–

I want the poppies to sprout.
I want the daisies to grow.
I want the dandelions to blow in the wind.
I want to bloom again without fear of
The frost returning.

But I guess that's just seasonal New England.

And I truly do love the space our winters take up,
And how green can only mean life
If death comes shortly before,
And threatens to appear at any moment.

Truly, I love living on the edge of breaking–
–toothy smile that might crack,
laughter that might get lost,
songs to dance to–
It is all quite exciting,

Because it is all quite scary.

Trembling, I say–
–i don't think i want to skip ahead–
I'll lay in bed and wait for my alarm,

Watch the days become big, red exes
On my calendar,
Until the circled box approaches;
I'll watch the circle get its own line
Drawn through it.

Independence does not feel as lonely
As I expected it to.

Truly, I think I can get used to this,

That is, until it changes,
And when it does–
–i will not be ready–

Because what would be the fun in that?

things i find perfect

My mother's smile
My father's hats
They nurture love through
Experiencing the world
And close the door on all
The growing pains threatening to enter.

The journey told in messages,
Scrolling back to the first year,
The glances of a friend,
Whose laugh becomes as loud through blue bubbles
As it is in person
We can all hear your joy,
And we appreciate the sound

I don't feel alone amongst the willows,
Whose heads rest on my shoulders,
Whose heart beats skip to catch up to mine,
Whose words are sidewalk chalk,
Intriguing yet amusing
Childlike in nature, bursting with dreams
That I hope will never be swallowed up
Amongst the leaves in the fall.

Autumn in New England,
The delicate balance between
Heat and heavy snow
When bright colors precede
The darkness settling in on the world,

Tucking my lively soul into bed.

The gap tooth of my dog,
When his tongue sticks out at me

His fur stands wildly on end
As he rolls in the grass,
And I join him, finding spirit
In our tethered lives.

The ache of muscles
As I work them to death
And watch, miraculously,
As they thank me for my effort

It's a journey to the finish line
And I intend to leap long before
The medal is in sight.

There is perfection in the little things,
When I don't begin to pick them apart

I think, for a while,
I could stand by and watch the little things
Grow to build a life

Only to find it staring back at me
Through the mirror.

We are what we find.
We become what we take.

roaming

The seatbelt sign sings.
I lock in, breathe deep.
Prepare for the journey ahead,
Resting my head against my hand, with
My elbows on the cool metal of the armrests.

I long for my home,
Its soft pillows, its comfortable safety,
And then I smile

Because the plane begins to roll
And roll and roll

And my head hurts
And my stomach hurts
And the muscles around my mouth hurt
From smiling.

Empty with no food,
But full of hopeful promise.

The sun is high before it is low,
I can not see it from my window anymore.
The sun is low before it rises,

And then the world blooms before me,
And I smile,

Because sailboats crowd the oceans,
Carried by gusts of wind.
Because mountains of green stretch before me,
Specks of orange houses scattered across,
Holding the lives of many, safe within their walls.

I am so far from home,
And yet I have never felt closer.

Breathe deep, breathe sure,
Lock in, the seatbelt will hold you steady,

But then you must fly free.

footprints

I want to do something of note!
Be someone of power,

Who shimmers when they shake
And never breaks when they fall
And builds bridges where they begin to sink
And rekindles fires where they feel ashes

I want to bring the world to its full!
Trace the whole circumference of this circle

Round and round
I'll dance across continents
Swim across the Atlantic
Walk barefoot along the Equator
      Twirl in the clouds
Be amongst the breeze as it brings
The world to fruition.

To me, this is a life unwasted.

people watching

The sun glows, as it meets
The edges of the universe.
Pebbles crunch, as my tires
Fold over them.
The fingers fanning, waving to me
As I turn to leave.

Humans are delicate.
Balanced in the eyes of one another,
Bound by a single thread that
Weaves its way through the centerpiece
That is our world.

The plain road, illuminated by the man,
Leaning over, holding his son's hand.
The high balcony, protecting the love of
Two souls, swaying to Earth's songs.
The only bird, wings tucked into its body
As it perches on the thin wire, watching
Our lives unfold.

Humans are vessels that only open
If you know the magic word.
I wish to ease into the shoes I must fill,
If blisters sprout, I let them grow
Because only then can the dictionary
Open to the right page.

The book, wrapped in ribbon, is passed
Through stories born from desert sand.
The rainstorm, where we dance to feel
Thunder rumbling through our rib cages and
Where we cry to feel lightning

Running through our veins.
The bodies, wrapped around one another,
Tangled limbs squeezing until we must
Let go and carry on.

Humans are lonely minds
Aiding swollen hearts.
Beats that never match unless
Laughter is the medicine.

The spark, that fizzles out only to
Explode in my blurry vision.
The text, emboldened to express
What could never rhyme.
The smile, which I fear will fade
But, I have the smallest inkling, it will only grow.

Humans are hopeful beasts.
When we sprain our ankles,
We carry them in the palm of our hands
Until they are well enough to walk again.

The photos, a rebirth of feelings
I thought I could escape,
And carrying words
I will never be able to form

But, oh, how humans are determined to fail
Just for a sliver of moon,
Imposing peace on all those who
Bask in its imaginary face.

peace by peace

Maybe it will all be okay in the end.

Maybe the sun will rise tomorrow
Maybe the oceans will never dry
The rivers will freeze so we can skate across
The rain won't flood and carry me away
The wind won't break me to bits, and
Swallow all of my fragmented parts.

But if they do,

I am glad I got to lay, spread among the grass,
The sky pouring onto me, all its anguish
Splashing in the puddles I stomp through,

I am glad I got to throw pebbles into the fire pit
Scratching secret messages into each large stepping stone,

I am glad I got to take photos on my front porch
And dress up for Halloween
And build mini snowmen because my fingers
Were so frozen, but it was the first
Sticky snow of the season,

I am glad I got to run into the world headfirst
Digging worms from the flower beds
Raising frogs I found in a pond,

I am glad the world has not come to an end
Quite yet,

I still sit in my backyard
Listening to soft music play as I read

Spread out among the grass,

I still have trouble with the gate
And sing as I kick it open,

I still feel every moment of me
In every corner of this home,

Perhaps the world ends when I leave,

I am glad that these are the pieces I keep
The souvenirs following me through life,
Which I can hear in the tickle of the wind
As it blows me from here to there,

Wherever that may be,

About The Author

Cecelia Allentuck is an 18 year old poet and author from Longmeadow, Massachusetts. For as long as she can remember she has loved storytelling – whether through short novels, poems, theater, or slam poetry– and after so many years of telling the same old stories to her parents, she thought she would branch out and share them with the world!

When she isn't writing, she can be found curled up with her dog reading a good book, on a run, singing and dancing, or just simply eating fruit and contemplating life.

www.ingramcontent.com/pod-product-compliance
Lightning Source LLC
Chambersburg PA
CBHW050728010526
44107CB00009B/774